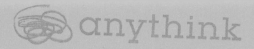

Food Chains and Webs

Mountain
Food Chains

Angela Royston

Heinemann
LIBRARY

Chicago, Illinois

© 2015 Heinemann Library
an imprint of Capstone Global Library, LLC
Chicago, Illinois

To contact Capstone Global Library, please
call 800-747-4992, or visit our web site
www.capstonepub.com

Edited by Claire Throp, Diyan Leake, and
Helen Cox-Cannons
Designed by Joanna Malivoire and
Philippa Jenkins
Original illustrations © Capstone Global
Library Ltd 2014
Picture research by Elizabeth Alexander and
Tracy Cummins
Production by Victoria Fitzgerald
Originated by Capstone Global Library Ltd
Printed and bound in China by Leo Paper Group

18 17 16 15 14
10 9 8 7 6 5 4 3 2 1

**Library of Congress Cataloging-in-
Publication Data**
Royston, Angela, 1945- author.
  Mountain food chains / Angela Royston.
    pages cm.—(Food chains and webs)
  Includes bibliographical references and index.
  ISBN 978-1-4846-0519-6 (hb)—ISBN
978-1-4846-0526-4 (pb) 1. Mountain
ecology—Juvenile literature. 2. Food chains
(Ecology)—Juvenile literature. 3. Mountain
animals—Juvenile literature. 4. Wildlife
conservation—Juvenile literature. I. Title.
  QH541.5.M65
  577.5'3—dc23   2013040533

Acknowledgments
We would like to thank the following for
permission to reproduce photographs: Alamy
pp. 10 (© imagebroker), 11a, 25 wolf (© Maciej
Wojtkowiak), 17a (© Juniors Bildarchiv GmbH),
18 (© Alaska Stock/John R. Delapp), 19 (©
WILDLIFE GmbH), 20 (© Roger Eritja), 23c
(© Mariano Garcia), 27 (© franzfoto.com),
28 (© Realimage); FLPA pp. 17c (Richard
Becker), 17d (Reinhard Hölzl/Imagebroker);
Photoshot p. 21 (© Bruce Coleman); Science
Photo Library p. 23a (SCIMAT); Shutterstock
pp. 1 (© momanuma), 4 (© Smit), 5 (© Diane
Garcia), 7 (© Arsgera), 8 (© Jim David), 9 (©
visceralimage), 11b, 25 sheep (© karamysh),
11c, 25 grass (© f9photos), 12 (© Patrick Poendl),
13 (© BergeImLicht), 14, 25 leopard (© Dennis
Donohue), 15 (© Critterbiz), 16 (© Yuriy Kulik),
17b (© Wolfgang Kruck), 22 (© Itay.G), 23b (©
Jarous), 23d (© Christian Vinces), 23e (© Ammit
Jack), 24, 25 vulture (© Hedrus), 25 earthworm
(© hsagencia), 25 hare (© Peter Wey), 25 ibex
(© USBFCO), 26 (© Kane513), 29 (© Hung
Chung Chih).

Cover photograph of mountain goats in Israel
reproduced with permission of Shutterstock
(© vblinov).

We would like to thank Michael Bright for his
invaluable help in the preparation of this book.

Contents

Some words are shown in bold, **like this.**
You can find out what they mean by
looking in the glossary.

High Mountains

Mountains are the highest places in the world. The air becomes colder and thinner the higher you go.

The tops of high mountains are covered with snow all year round.

Wild goats are at home on steep mountainsides.

Only special types of plants and animals can live on these cold, windy slopes. This book looks at how mountain animals survive and what they find to eat.

Where Are the Highest Mountains?

This map shows the world's highest mountain ranges. The plants on the lowest slopes are just like those in the countryside nearby. Different plants and fewer plants grow higher up. There are no plants on icy mountaintops!

Mountains are marked on the map in purple.

The Pyrenees

The Alps

The Caucasus

The Atlas Mountains

The Himalaya Mountains

Rocky Mountains

Appalachian Mountains

Mount Everest

The Equator

The Ethiopian Highlands

Andes Mountains

Highest mountain

The highest mountain in the world is Mount
Everest. It is in the Himalayas and is 29,029 feet
(8,848 meters) tall.

What Is a Food Chain?

All living things need food to survive. This is because food provides the **energy** they need to grow and stay alive.

A mule deer eats leaves in the Rocky Mountains.

A cougar hunts for mule deer and other animals.

A **food chain** shows what eats what. It also shows how energy passes along the chain from one living thing to another.

A Himalayan Food Chain

Wolves and wild sheep both live in the Himalayan Mountains. The wolf gets **energy** by eating the sheep, and the sheep gets energy from eating the grass. Neither animal would survive without the grass!

The Himalayas

Food chain

A wolf creeps up on a wild sheep and then it pounces

Wild sheep feed on grass on steep mountain slopes

Grass grows in the Himalayas

Plants and the Sun

Both the sheep and the wolf get **energy** from plants. All green plants make their own food, and so they are called **producers**.

Green plants cannot survive without the Sun.

This butterfly is sipping nectar from a mountain flower.

Green plants use energy from sunlight to produce sugary food in their leaves. This sugary liquid then feeds the whole plant.

Animal Consumers

All animals are called **consumers** because they get their food from the environment. **Carnivores**, such as wolves and snow leopards, hunt and eat other animals.

A snow leopard is a carnivore.

A black bear is an omnivore.

Sheep and animals that eat plants are called **herbivores**. Some animals, such as foxes and black bears, eat both plants and animals. They are called **omnivores**.

An Alpine Food Chain

Many **food chains** have just three links, but the one on page 17 has four links. These animals live in the Alps in Europe. **Energy** passes from the plants through the caterpillar, to the marmot and the red fox.

The Alps in Europe

Food chain

Red foxes hunt marmots

An Alpine marmot eats a caterpillar

A small, pearl-bordered fritillary caterpillar eats violet leaves

Violet

Top Predators

Some animals, such as bears and birds of prey, are not hunted by other animals. They are always at the top of their **food chains**. There are fewer top **predators** than other animals, because predators would starve if they caught all their prey.

A brown, or "grizzly," bear is a top predator in the Rocky Mountains.

This golden eagle is about to grab its prey.

Some predators are also **scavengers**. They feed on animals that are already dead. Golden eagles and foxes are scavengers.

Dealing with Leftovers

Scavengers, such as foxes and some eagles, begin the job of recycling dead animals. Insects, fungi, and bacteria are **decomposers**, and they finish off the job.

All types of fungi are decomposers.

A snow flea is a decomposer and an insect, but it is not a real flea. Its proper name is a springtail.

Decomposers feed on the remains of animals and plants, breaking them up into tiny pieces. The tiny pieces become part of the soil, and so they help plants to grow.

An Andean Food Chain

The **food chain** on page 23, from the Andes in South America, includes a **scavenger** and a **decomposer**. **Energy** passes from the plants to the vicuña and then to the puma. Condors feed on dead pumas. Bacteria decompose the leftovers.

The Andes Mountains

Food chain

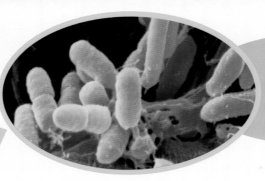

Bacteria are decomposers

A condor is a scavenger

A puma hunts vicuñas

A vicuña eats plants

Plants grow in the Andes

Food Webs

Most animals eat many different things, although **carnivores** always eat meat, and **herbivores** always eat plants. In any **habitat**, the **food chains** crisscross to form a **food web**. The food web on page 25 is from the Himalayas.

A vulture is a **scavenger**. The food web on page 25 shows what it eats.

Food web

vulture

snow leopard

Tibetan wolf

ibex

mountain hare

argali sheep

grass

earthworm

Broken Chains

Some **food chains** rely on particular animals. In the Rocky Mountains, gray wolves hunt elk. When the gray wolves began to disappear, the number of elk increased. The elk destroyed the willow trees along the riverbanks.

This gray wolf lives in Yellowstone National Park.

A beaver eats grass as well as willow.

Beavers eat willow and use it to build their dams. Because the elk destroyed the willow in this area, the beavers died out. However, when gray wolves were brought back, the beavers returned.

Protecting Food Chains

People now live higher up mountainsides than they did before. Mountain animals are being pushed out by farms and villages. Giant pandas are in danger of becoming extinct because there are fewer patches of mountain forest for them to live in.

Many tourists and climbers visit high mountains.

Most wild pandas now live in nature reserves in China.

People protect pandas by making **nature reserves.** At the same time, the other animals that live there, such as clouded leopards and golden eagles, are protected, too.

Glossary

carnivore animal that eats only the meat of other animals

consumer living thing, particularly an animal, that feeds on other living things, such as plants and other animals

decomposer living thing, such as an earthworm, fungus, or bacterium, that breaks up the remains of plants and animals and turns them into soil

energy power needed to do something, such as move, breathe, or swallow

food chain diagram that shows how energy passes from plants to different animals

food web diagram that shows how different plants and animals in a habitat are linked by what they eat

habitat place where something lives

herbivore animal that eats only plants

nature reserve area in which plants and animals are protected

omnivore animal that eats plants and animals

predator animal that hunts other animals for food

producer living thing, such as a plant, that makes its own food

scavenger animal that feeds off the flesh and remains of dead animals

Find Out More

Books

Facthound offers a safe, fun way to find web sites related to this book. All the sites on Facthound have been researched by our staff.

Here's all you do:

Visit www.facthound.com

Type in this code: 9781484605196

Web sites

www.nps.gov/romo/naturescience/animals.htm
Learn more about the different kinds of animals that live in Rocky Mountain National Park in Colorado.

wwf.panda.org/about_our_earth/ecoregions/about/habitat_types/ habitats/mountains
The World Wildlife Fund site includes information about mountains. Click on "giant panda" to learn more about this endangered animal.

www.sheppardsoftware.com/content/animals/kidscorner/ foodchain/foodchain.htm
This web site includes fun games and information about food chains.

Index